Contents

Introduction

The contents of this book are based upon the National Science Education Standards for Grade 1. These standards include (A) Unifying Concepts and Processes, (B) Science as Inquiry, (C) Physical Science, (D) Life Science, (E) Earth and Space Science, (F) Science and Technology, (G) Science in Personal and Social Perspectives, and (H) History and Nature of Science.

This book will help teachers, students, parents, and tutors. Teachers can use this book either to introduce or review a topic in their science classroom. Students will find the book useful in reviewing the major concepts in science. Parents can use this book to help their children with topics that may be posing a problem in the classroom. Tutors can use this book as a basis for their lessons and for assigning questions and activities.

This book includes nine lessons that focus on the nine major concepts presented in the content standards: Physical Science, Life Science, and Earth and Space Science. The lessons also cover the sixteen major concepts presented in the other standards. A table on page 4 provides a correlation between the contents of each lesson and the National Science Education Standards.

Before beginning the book, the reader can check his or her knowledge of the content by completing the *Assessment*. The *Assessment* consists of questions that deal with the content standards. This will allow the reader to determine how much he or she knows about a particular concept before beginning to read about it. The *Assessment* may also serve as a way of leading the reader to a specific lesson that may be of special interest.

Each lesson follows the same sequence in presenting the material. A list of *Key Terms* is always provided at the beginning of each lesson. This list includes all the boldfaced terms and their definitions presented in the same order that they are introduced in the lesson. The reader can develop a sense of the lesson content by glancing through the *Key Terms*. Each lesson then provides background information about the concept. This information is divided into several sections. Each section is written so that the reader is not overwhelmed with details. Rather, the reader is guided through the concept in a logical sequence. Each lesson then moves on to a *Review*. This section consists of several multiple-choice questions designed to check if the reader has retained information that was covered in the lesson.

Each lesson then moves on to a series of activities. These activities are designed to check the reader's understanding of the information. Some activities extend the lesson by presenting additional information. The activities are varied so as not to be boring. For example, reading passages about interesting and unusual findings are included. Questions to check reading comprehension are then asked.

The last activity in each lesson is an experiment. Each experiment has been designed so that the required items are easy to locate and can usually be found in most households. Care has been taken to avoid the use of any dangerous materials or chemicals. However, an adult should always be present when a student is conducting an experiment. In some cases, the experimental procedure reminds students that adult supervision is required. Before beginning any experiment, an adult should review the list of materials and the procedure. In this way, the adult will be aware of any situations that may need special attention. The adult should review the safety issues before the experiment is begun. The adult may want to check a laboratory manual for specific safety precautions that should be followed when doing an experiment, such as wearing safety goggles and never touching or tasting chemicals.

The book then follows with a *Science Fair* section. Information is presented on how to conduct and present a science fair project. In some cases, the experiment at the end of a lesson can serve as the basis for a science fair project. Additional suggestions are also provided with advice on how to choose an award-winning science fair project.

A *Glossary* is next. This section lists all the boldfaced terms in alphabetical order and indicates the page on which the term is used. The book concludes with an *Answer Key*, which gives the answers to all the activity questions, including the experiment.

This book has been designed and written so that teachers, students, parents, and tutors will find it easy to use and follow. Most importantly, students will benefit from this book by achieving at a higher level in class and on standardized tests.

National Science Education Standards

Standard A: UNIFYING CONCEPTS AND PROCESSES

A1 Systems, order, and organization
A2 Evidence, models, and explanation
A3 Change, constancy, and measurement
A4 Evolution and equilibrium
A5 Form and function

Standard B: SCIENCE AS INQUIRY

B1 Abilities necessary to do scientific inquiry
B2 Understanding about scientific inquiry

Standard C: PHYSICAL SCIENCE

C1 Properties of objects and materials
C2 Position and motion of objects
C3 Light, heat, electricity, and magnetism

Standard D: LIFE SCIENCE

D1 Characteristics of organisms
D2 Life cycles of organisms
D3 Organisms and environments

Standard E: EARTH AND SPACE SCIENCE

E1 Properties of earth materials
E2 Objects in the sky
E3 Changes in earth and sky

Standard F: SCIENCE AND TECHNOLOGY

F1 Abilities to distinguish between natural objects and objects made by humans
F2 Abilities of technological design
F3 Understanding about science and technology

Standard G: SCIENCE IN PERSONAL AND SOCIAL PERSPECTIVES

G1 Personal health
G2 Characteristics and changes in populations
G3 Types of resources
G4 Changes in environments
G5 Science and technology in local challenges

Standard H: HISTORY AND NATURE OF SCIENCE

H1 Science as a human endeavor

National Science Education Standards
Science I, SV 9781419034299

Correlation to National Science Education Standards

Unit 1: Physical Science
Lesson 1: Properties of Objects and Materials

Background Information A3, C1
Review C1
Kinds of Matter C1
Float or Sink C1
Submarines C1, F2
Experiment: Which One Floats on Top? B2, C1

Lesson 2: Position and Motion of Objects

Background Information A3, C2
Review C2
Types of Motion C2
Comparing Surfaces C2
Curling A1, C2, H1
Experiment: Making Things Move B1, C2

Lesson 3: Light, Heat, Electricity, and Magnetism

Background Information A2, C3
Review C3
All About Energy C3
Lights All Around C3
Magnetic Forces C3
Magnetic Trains C3, F3, G5
Experiment: Bending Light A2, B2, C3

Unit 2: Life Science
Lesson 4: Characteristics of Organisms

Background Information A5, D1, G2
Review D1
Sensing Your Surroundings D1
Alive or Not D1
Sounds Animals Hear A5, D1, G2
Experiment: Using Your Senses A2, B2, D1

Lesson 5: Life Cycles of Organisms

Background Information A3, D2
Review D2

Growing and Changing D2
Caterpillars D2
Mix and Match D2
Ostriches A5, D2
Experiment: Butterfly Life Cycle B2, A4, D2

Lesson 6: Organisms and Environments

Background Information A1, D3, G4
Review D3
Animal Environments D3
What Would You Do? D3
Cold Desert D3, G2, G4
Experiment: Animal Habitats A1, B2, D3

Unit 3: Earth and Space Science
Lesson 7: Properties of Earth Materials

Background Information A5, E1, F1, G3
Review E1
Earth's Materials E1
A Rock Collection E1
Plants on the Menu E1, G3
All About Air E1, G3
Growing Plants Without Soil E1, F3, G5
Experiment: A River Model A2, B2, E1, G4

Lesson 8: Objects in the Sky

Background Information A2, E2, F1
Review E2
Twinkle, Twinkle E2
Life Cycle of a Star A4, E2
Experiment: By the Light
of the Moon A2, B2, E2

Lesson 9: Changes in Earth and Sky

Background Information A3, E3
Review E3
Changes in the Sky E3
The Seasons E3
Time Zones E3, G5, H1
Experiment: Sunrise to Sunset A3, B2, E3

Correlation to National Science Education Standards
Science I, SV 9781419034299

Assessment

Darken the circle by the best answer.

Lesson 1

1. Which type of matter is milk?

(A) solid

(B) liquid

(C) gas

Lesson 2

2. What is a force?

(A) a push or pull

(B) a type of matter

(C) a living thing

Lesson 3

3. What happens when light hits a mirror?

(A) The light bends.

(B) The light bounces off the mirror.

(C) The light passes through the mirror.

Lesson 4

4. What is something all living things need?

(A) clothes

(B) water

(C) sunlight

Assessment
Science 1, SV 9781419034299

Assessment, page 2

Lesson 5

5. Which of these animals hatches?

(A) bird

(B) kitten

(C) puppy

Lesson 6

6. In which environment does a shark live?

(A) desert

(B) rain forest

(C) ocean

Lesson 7

7. Which of these is a natural resource?

(A) soil

(B) car

(C) television

Lesson 8

8. What is the moon?

(A) a rock

(B) a star

(C) a planet

Lesson 9

9. Which season comes right after summer?

(A) fall

(B) winter

(C) spring

Lesson 1 Properties of Objects and Materials

Matter is all around you.
Shirts and shoes are matter.
Gloves and hats are matter, too.
So are you and your friends.
Anything that takes up space is matter.

Key Terms

matter—everything around you

solid—matter that keeps its shape

liquid—matter that flows

float—to stay on top of a liquid

sink—to drop to the bottom of a liquid

dissolve—to mix with a liquid

gas—matter that does not have its own shape or size

change—to make different

Solids

Pick up a coin.

Hold the coin in your hand.

Put the coin on your desk.

The coin does not change shape.

The coin is a solid.

A **solid** is matter that keeps its shape.

The shape does not change even when the

solid moves.

Solids can be different.

They can have different colors.

Solids can have different shapes.

You can sort solids into groups.

The blocks below are sorted by shape.

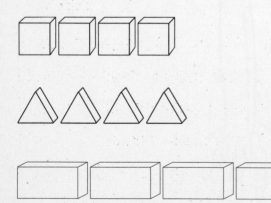

Liquids

Water flows when you pour it.
Water is a liquid.
A **liquid** is matter that flows.

The shape of a liquid can change.
A liquid changes to match the shape of its container.
The size of the liquid stays the same.

Liquids flow differently.
Honey flows slowly.
It is very thick.
Water flows fast.
It is thin.
Some liquids are thick.
Others are thin.
Thin liquids flow faster than thick liquids.

Lesson 1, Properties of Objects and Materials
Science 1, SV 9781419034299

Mixing Liquids

Pour oil into water.

The oil does not mix.

Pour vinegar into water.

The vinegar mixes.

Some liquids mix with water.

Others do not.

Sink or Float

A cork will **float** in water.

It stays on top of water.

A stone will **sink**.

It drops to the bottom.

Some objects float in a liquid.

Others sink.

The shape of an object can help it float or sink.

A sheet of foil floats on top of water.

If you crumple it into a ball, it sinks.

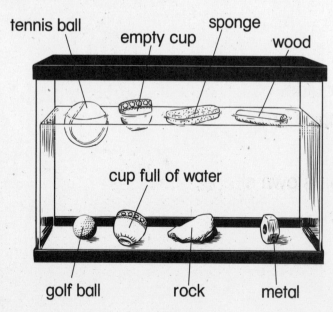

tennis ball   sponge

empty cup   wood

cup full of water

golf ball   rock   metal

Lesson 1, Properties of Objects and Materials
Science 1, SV 9781419034299

Dissolving

What happens if you add sugar to warm water?

The sugar will mix well, or **dissolve**.

Some solids do not dissolve in a liquid.

Sand will not dissolve in water.

Some solids dissolve better in a hot liquid than

in a cold liquid.

More sugar dissolves in hot tea than in iced tea.

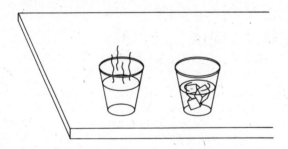

Gases

You are surrounded by air. Air is made up

of gases.

A **gas** is matter that does not have its own shape.

A gas does not keep its size, either.

It spreads out to fill its container.

You cannot see many gases.
You can feel them or see what they do.
Blow on your hand. You can feel the moving air.

You can see what happens when some gases
mix with liquids.
Bubbles in a liquid are made of gases.

You can see what gases do.
Blow air into a balloon.
You can see that air takes up space.
What happens when the balloon pops?

Lesson 1, Properties of Objects and Materials
Science 1, SV 9781419034299

Changing Objects

You can paint a wood car.

You can cut a sheet of paper.

You can bend a wire.

When you paint or cut or bend, you change an object.

To **change** an object is to make it different.

Another way to change an object is to freeze it.

Freezing changes liquid water into solid ice.

When the solid ice melts, it changes back into a liquid.

Lesson 1, Properties of Objects and Materials
Science 1, SV 9781419034299

Lesson 1

Review

Darken the circle by the best answer.

1. Which of these is a type of matter?

Ⓐ thoughts

Ⓑ music

Ⓒ toys

2. Which type of matter is a desk?

Ⓐ liquid

Ⓑ solid

Ⓒ gas

3. What happens when a liquid is poured into a new container?

Ⓐ It changes shape.

Ⓑ It changes size.

Ⓒ It changes color.

4. An object stays at the top of a liquid. This object

Ⓐ sinks.

Ⓑ dissolves.

Ⓒ floats.

5. Which of these means changing an object?

Ⓐ measuring it

Ⓑ looking at it

Ⓒ breaking it in half

Lesson 1   **Kinds of Matter**

Match the words and their meanings. Write the letter of the meaning on the line next to the word.

_____ 1. change

_____ 2. dissolve

_____ 3. float

_____ 4. gas

_____ 5. liquid

_____ 6. matter

_____ 7. sink

_____ 8. solid

a. matter that keeps its shape and size

b. matter that flows

c. matter that does not have its own shape or size

d. to mix with a liquid

e. to drop to the bottom of a liquid

f. everything around you

g. to make different

h. to stay on top of a liquid

Lesson 1

Float or Sink

Look at the pictures. Write <u>float</u> if the object floats. Write <u>sink</u> if the object sinks.

1. _____

2. _____

3. _____

4. _____

Lesson 1, Float or Sink
Science 1, SV 9781419034299

Lesson 1
Submarines

Read the following passage. Then answer the questions.

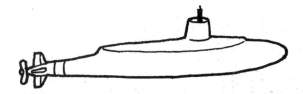

A submarine is like a boat.
It is made to go under water.

A submarine uses special tanks.
These tanks are called ballast tanks.

The submarine starts on the surface.
The tanks are filled with air.

Then water is put into the tanks.
This makes the submarine sink.

When air is put back into the tanks, water
is pushed out.
The submarine floats back up.

Lesson 1, Submarines
Science 1, SV 9781419034299

1. Where do submarines go?

   (A) in air

   (B) in dirt

   (C) in water

2. Why do submarines have ballast tanks?

   (A) to paint them

   (B) to help them move up and down

   (C) to make them move backwards

3. How does a submarine sink?

   (A) It takes on more people.

   (B) It makes more air.

   (C) It fills its tanks with water.

4. Why is water pushed out of a submarine's ballast tanks?

   (A) to make it float to the ocean's surface

   (B) to make more room inside

   (C) to make it heavier

Lesson 1, Submarines
Science 1, SV 9781419034299

Lesson 1   Experiment: Which One Floats on Top?

You have to shake orange juice.

Do you know why?

Some parts of the orange juice sink.

Other parts float to the top.

You need to mix them together.

In this activity, you will find out which liquids float

in others.

What You Will Need

1 paper cup filled halfway with water

1 paper cup filled halfway with corn syrup

1 paper cup filled halfway with vegetable oil

clear plastic container or large measuring cup

food coloring

stirring rod, straw, or spoon

Procedure

1. Add a few drops of red food coloring to the
   water. Stir.

2. Add a few drops blue food coloring to the corn
   syrup. Stir.

3. Slowly pour the vegetable oil into the container.

4. Gently pour the corn syrup into the container.
   Do not stir.

Experiment: Which One Floats on Top? (cont'd.)

5. Gently pour the water into the container. Do not stir.

6. Wait several minutes. Look at the liquids in the container.

Analysis

1. Which liquid sank to the bottom?

_ _

_ _

2. Which liquid was in the middle?

_ _

_ _

3. Which liquid floated on top?

_ _

_ _

Experiment: Which One Floats on Top? (cont'd.)

Conclusion

1. Which sample of liquid was the heaviest?

_____

- -

_____

2. Which liquid was the lightest?

_____

- -

_____

3. Do you think the results would change if you poured the water first, then the oil, then the corn syrup?

_____

- -

_____

Lesson 2 Position and Motion of Objects

A **force** is a push or a pull.
You can pull a wagon.
This brings it closer to you.
You can push a door open.
This makes it go away from you.

force—a push or a pull

curve—a bend

speed—how fast or slow an object moves

motion—moving from one place to another

friction—a force that acts against motion

surface—the top or outside of something

Moving

A push or a pull can make things move.

You push a ball.

You pull on a suitcase.

A push or a pull can also make things stop
moving.

They make things change direction.

Someone throws a ball to you.

You can push it with a bat.

Your push makes the ball stop.

Then it makes it change direction and move away.

Lesson 2, Position and Motion of Objects
Science 1, SV 9781419034299

Ways Things Move

Things move in different ways.
Some things move in straight path.
A car might drive in a straight path.

Some things move in a **curve**.
A curve is a bend.
A car may curve along its path.

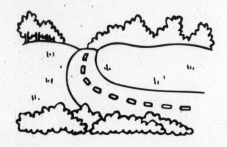

Some things spin.
A top spins around in a circle.
Some things move back and forth.
You move back and forth on a swing.

Lesson 2, Position and Motion of Objects
Science 1, SV 9781419034299

Some things move fast.

Other things move slowly.

Two birds leave the same branch at the same time.

One bird flies ahead. It moves faster than the other.

It has a faster **speed**. An object's speed is how fast or slow it moves.

fast

slow

A force makes an object move.

Moving from one place to another is **motion**.

An object will keep moving straight unless a force changes its motion.

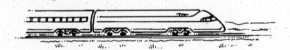

You kick a ball.

The ball rolls across a field of grass.

It comes to a stop.

What changed the ball's motion?

The answer is friction.

Friction is a force that acts against motion.

A **surface** is the top of something.

The top of a floor or desk is its surface.

Some surfaces are smooth.

Others are rough.

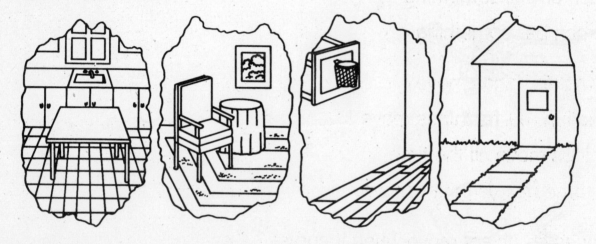

A rough surface has more friction than a smooth one.

Grass has a rough surface.

There is friction between the ball and the grass.

Friction changes the motion of the ball.

Friction makes the ball stop.

Lesson 2   **Review**

Darken the circle by the best answer.

1. What do you do when you apply a force?

   Ⓐ tell someone to do something

   Ⓑ push or pull something

   Ⓒ remember something

2. What makes things move?

   Ⓐ Friction makes things move.

   Ⓑ Things move all the time.

   Ⓒ A force makes things move.

3. How does an object move when it curves?

   Ⓐ It moves along a bend.

   Ⓑ It moves back and forth.

   Ⓒ It spins in a circle.

4. What does an object's speed tell you?

   Ⓐ how big the object is

   Ⓑ how fast the object moves

   Ⓒ where the object is

5. Which surface has the least friction?

   Ⓐ a thick rug

   Ⓑ a road made of rock

   Ⓒ a smooth floor

Lesson 2

Types of Motion

The pictures show different types of motion. Use the words below to name each type of motion. Write the correct word next to each picture.

| zigzag | curve | spin | back and forth | straight |

1. _____

2. _____

3. _____

4. _____

5. _____

Lesson 2, Types of Motion
Science 1, SV 9781419034299

Lesson 2
Comparing Surfaces

Gather several different materials. You can use surfaces in the room. Try to find sandpaper, carpet, tile, marble, or wood. Use whatever surfaces you can find. They must be flat.

Feel each surface with your fingers. Write one or two words that describe the surface.

Surface	How It Feels

Place a toy car on the first surface. Give it a gentle push. Watch how it moves.

Do the same thing for each surface.

On which surface does the car move the farthest distance?

_____

- -

_____

On which surface does the car move the shortest distance?

_____

- -

_____

Lesson 2   **Curling**

Read the following passage. Then answer the questions.

Have you ever watched a sport called curling?

This sport is played on ice.

A team pushes a stone on the ice.

The players try to get the stone into a circle.

The players use brooms to sweep in front of
the stone.

The sweeping melts the ice a little.

It makes the surface more slippery.

This means there is less friction.

The stone slides farther.

1. Where does curling happen?

   Ⓐ in water

   Ⓑ on sand

   Ⓒ on ice

2. Why do players sweep the ice?

   Ⓐ to make more friction

   Ⓑ to lower friction

   Ⓒ to make a hole in the ice

Lesson 2

Experiment: Making Things Move

Picture a car without wheels.
It would not move very well.
In this activity, you will compare
rolling with sliding.

What You Will Need

10 pencils
several books
1 large rubber band

Procedure

1. Place several books in a stack.

2. Wrap the rubber band around the books.

3. Hold onto the rubber band. Gently pull it until
   the books move.

4. Look at how far the rubber band stretches.

5. Arrange the pencils in a row.

6. Place the stack of books on top of the pencils.

7. Repeat Steps 3 and 4.

Experiment: Making Things Move (cont'd.)

Analysis

1. Did the rubber band stretch more with or without the pencils?

_____

- -

_____

2. What part of a car is most like the pencils you used?

_____

- -

_____

Conclusion

You pulled on the books to make them move.
You used a force.
How do wheels change the amount of force you
need to move something?

_____

- -

_____

- -

_____

Lesson 3 Light, Heat, Electricity, and Magnetism

You wake up in the night.
What do you do if you want to see?
You turn on the light.
Light lets you see things.

Light is a type of energy.
Energy can make things change.

A lot of the light you use comes from
the sun.
Light also comes from lamps and flashlights.
Some light comes from candles and
campfires.

Key Terms

energy—the ability to make things change

circuit—a path that electricity flows through

pole—a place where a magnet is strongest

attract—to pull together

repel—to push apart

Light hits objects around you.
Light bounces off some objects.
Light bounces off a mirror.

Light goes through some objects.
Light goes through a window.

Some objects bend light.
If light hits an object at a slant, light will bend.
Light can bend when it passes through water.

Heat

Light is not the only energy that comes
from the sun.
The sun gives off heat, too.
Heat is another type of energy.

Heat moves from warmer objects to colder
objects.
Heat moves from warm water to cold ice cubes.
Heat moves from a warm rock to a cold lizard.

When heat moves to an object, the object gets
warmer.
When heat moves out of an object, the object
gets cooler.

Electricity

You want a radio to work.
You plug it into a wall socket.
Electricity moves into the radio.
The energy of the electricity makes the
radio work.

Lesson 3, Light, Heat, Electricity, and Magnetism
Science 1, SV 9781419034299

What if you are not near a wall socket?
You can use batteries.
A battery stores electrical energy.

Electricity flows in a **circuit**.
A circuit is a path that electricity follows.

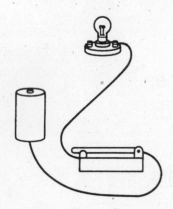

Magnets

Do you hang papers on your refrigerator?
You can use a magnet.
A magnet is something that pushes or pulls
metals.

Magnets can have different shapes.
Some magnets are stronger than others.

Lesson 3, Light, Heat, Electricity, and Magnetism
Science 1, SV 9781419034299

Every magnet has two **poles**.
A pole is a place where the magnet is strongest.

One pole is called a north pole.
The other is called a south pole.

Two poles that are different **attract** each other.
This means they pull together.

Two poles that are the same **repel** each other.
This means they push each other away.

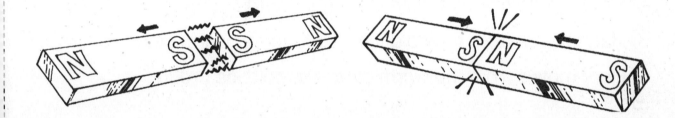

Lesson 3   **Review**

Darken the circle by the best answer.

I. What happens when light hits water at a slant?

(A) The light disappears.

(B) The light bends.

(C) The light changes color.

2. What happens when you leave ice cream on a table?

(A) Heat moves from the cold ice cream to the table.

(B) Heat moves from the cold ice cream to the warm air.

(C) Heat moves from the warm air to the cold ice cream.

3. What does a battery do?

(A) It stores electrical energy.

(B) It makes things work without electricity.

(C) It makes things work without a circuit.

4. What are the poles of a magnet?

(A) the places where the magnet does not work

(B) the places where the magnet is strongest

(C) the places where the magnet bends

5. What happens when a magnet repels an object?

(A) The magnet breaks the object in half.

(B) The magnet pulls the object closer.

(C) The magnet pushes the object away.

Lesson 3

All About Energy

Write words to complete the sentences. Choose from the words in the box.

battery	bend	circuit
energy	heat	poles

1. The ability to make things change is called _____.

2. Light can _____ when it passes through water at a slant.

3. _____ is energy that moves from a warm object to a cooler one.

4. A _____ stores electrical energy.

5. Electricity flows through a path called a _____.

6. Every magnet has two parts called _____.

Lesson 3

Lights All Around

Light comes from many different things. Think of a room in your home. In the space below, draw everything that gives off light.

Be sure to include things that you might not think of right away. Think about clocks, refrigerators, and televisions. Show as many things as you can.

Lesson 3

Magnetic Forces

The pictures below show two sets of magnets. Draw arrows on each set to show if the magnets pull together or push apart. Then label the magnets <u>attract</u> or <u>repel</u>.

I.

| N   S | | S   N |

_____

- -

_____

2.

| N   S | | N   S |

_____

- -

_____

Lesson 3, Magnetic Forces
Science I, SV 9781419034299

Lesson 3   **Magnetic Trains**

Read the following passage. Then answer the questions.

A regular train moves on wheels.

The wheels fit on a track.

The train engine burns a fuel.

The fuel might be coal or diesel.

A new kind of train does not have an engine.

It does not have wheels.

It uses magnets to move.

Two magnets can push each other apart.

There are magnets in the train and in the track.

The magnets make the train float in air.

When the magnets are changed, the train
moves ahead.

These trains are called maglev trains.

These trains can move faster than other trains.

They are very quiet.

They do not burn fuel.

They do not have many parts to fix.

Magnetic Trains (cont'd.)

There are not many maglev trains.

They cost a lot of money to build.

They need special tracks.

Someday there may be more maglev trains.

1. What makes a maglev train go?

(A) heat

(B) light

(C) magnets

2. What is a good thing about maglev trains?

(A) They are quiet.

(B) They are heavy.

(C) They cost a lot of money.

3. What is a bad thing about maglev trains?

(A) They can carry lots of people.

(B) They need special tracks.

(C) They can move very fast.

Lesson 3, Magnetic Trains
Science 1, SV 9781419034299

Lesson 3

Experiment: Bending Light

Some things bend light.

In this activity, you will try to bend light.

What You Will Need

I penny   I foam cup   water

Procedure

1. Put the penny in the bottom of the foam cup.

2. Tape the penny to the cup so it does not move.

3. Put the cup on a table or desk.

4. Look at the penny. Move your head down until you cannot see it.

5. Have a partner slowly pour water into the cup.

6. Keep your head in the same place. Look for the penny.

Analysis

What blocked the penny when you moved your head down?

_____

- -

_____

Conclusion

What happened when your partner added water to the cup?

_____

- -

_____

Lesson 4 Characteristics of Organisms

Close your eyes.

Think of a smell you like.

Is it warm banana bread?

Maybe you smell a juicy orange.

Smell is one of your five **senses**.

You use your senses to find out about things.

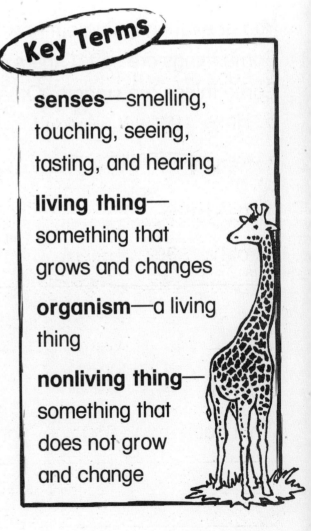

Key Terms

senses—smelling, touching, seeing, tasting, and hearing

living thing— something that grows and changes

organism—a living thing

nonliving thing— something that does not grow and change

Lesson 4, Characteristics of Organisms
Science 1, SV 9781419034299

You use sight to look at things.
You can see color and shape.
You can see how big or small things are.

You use touch to find out how things feel.
Some things are soft. Others are hard.
Some things are smooth. Others are rough.

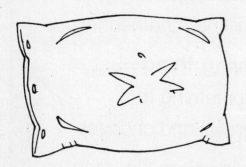

Lesson 4, Characteristics of Organisms
Science 1, SV 9781419034299

You use hearing to find out what sounds
things make.

A cat makes a quiet sound.

A horn makes a loud sound.

You use taste to find out about foods.

Some foods taste sweet. Others taste sour.

Some foods taste salty.

You use your senses to find out about things
around you.

Some things are **living**.

People are living things.

So are plants and animals.

Another name for a living thing is an **organism**.

Lesson 4, Characteristics of Organisms
Science 1, SV 9781419034299

Some things are **nonliving**.

Desks are nonliving.

Books and pencils are nonliving, too.

The world is full of living and nonliving things.

Lesson 4, Characteristics of Organisms
Science 1, SV 9781419034299

Living things have needs.

Think about the food you eat.

Living things need food.

Living things need water.

You need to drink water each day.

Living things need air.

You breathe air.

Living things grow and change.

You were once a small baby.

Now you are a child.

You have grown and changed.

Living things make new living things.

Dogs have puppies.

Cats have kittens.

All living things come from other living things.

Lesson 4, Characteristics of Organisms
Science 1, SV 9781419034299

Nonliving things do not need food.

They do not need water or air.

They do not grow.

Some things look like they are living,

but they are not.

Water in a river can move.

Water does not need food or air.

Water is nonliving.

A tree does not move, but it is living.

A tree needs food. It needs water and air.

A tree grows and changes.

Lesson 4

Darken the circle by the best answer.

1. Which of these is NOT one of your five senses?

(A) hearing

(B) tasting

(C) falling

2. Which of these is a living thing?

(A) water

(B) a stone

(C) a sunflower plant

3. What is something that all living things need?

(A) water

(B) money

(C) cars

4. What do all living things do?

(A) They move around.

(B) They change and grow.

(C) They turn green.

5. Which do nonliving things have in common?

(A) They do not need water or air.

(B) They have batteries.

(C) They are big.

Lesson 4

Sensing Your Surroundings

In the spaces below, draw something you can learn about with the sense listed.

For example, you might draw a flower for smelling and a bell for hearing. Come up with your own ideas.

SMELLING	HEARING	SEEING	TASTING	TOUCHING

Lesson 4   Alive or Not

Look at the pictures. Write <u>living</u> or <u>nonliving</u> under each picture.

1.

_____

- - - - - - - - - - - - - - -

_____

2.

_____

- - - - - - - - - - - - - - -

_____

3.

_____

- - - - - - - - - - - - - - -

_____

4.

_____

- - - - - - - - - - - - - - -

_____

5.
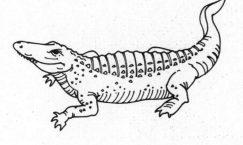

_____

- - - - - - - - - - - - - - -

_____

6.

_____

- - - - - - - - - - - - - - -

_____

Lesson 4, Alive or Not
Science 1, SV 9781419034299

Lesson 4   Sounds Animals Hear

Read the following passage. Then answer the questions.

You can make your voice sound high.
You can make your voice sound low.
Frequency describes how high or low a sound is.

There are many sounds that humans cannot hear.
The sounds are too high or too low.

Animals can hear sounds that humans cannot.
A dog whistle makes a sound that is very high.
A human cannot hear it, but a dog can.

Elephants make sounds that are very low.
Humans cannot hear them, but elephants can.

1. What is the frequency of a sound?

   (A) the thing that makes the sound

   (B) how high or low the sound is

   (C) how loud the sound is

2. Which sentence is true?

(A) Humans can only hear sounds with certain frequencies.

(B) Humans can hear every sound that is made by animals.

(C) Humans and animals cannot hear any of the same sounds.

3. Why can't humans hear a dog whistle?

(A) It does not make a sound.

(B) It makes a sound that is too low.

(C) It makes a sound that is too high.

4. Why can't humans hear sounds made by elephants?

(A) The sounds have a high frequency.

(B) The sounds have a low frequency.

(C) The sounds are not loud enough.

Lesson 4   Experiment: Using Your Senses

You use your senses to find out about things.
Seeing is only one of your senses.
In this activity, you will test your other senses.

What You Will Need

a partner

several foods (pickle, lemon, orange, cheese, candy)

several objects that can be used to make noises
    (triangle, dominoes, deck of cards, bell)

several objects with different feels (sandpaper, cotton ball)

blindfold

Procedure

1. Do not let your partner see the objects. Place a
   blindfold on your partner.

2. Hand your partner an object, such as a pickle.

3. Ask your partner to guess what the object is.
   Note: Be sure to tell your partner if it is safe to
   taste an object.

4. If an object can make a noise, make that noise
   for your partner.

5. Write down which senses your partner used.

6. Repeat Steps 2 to 5 for other objects.

Experiment: Using Your Senses (cont'd.)

Analysis

Object	Smell?	Touch?	Taste?	Hearing?

Conclusion

How do all your senses work together?

_____

_____

_____

_____

_____

_____

Lesson 5 Life Cycles of Organisms

Do you like baby animals?
Some baby animals are cute and fuzzy.
Others are big and tough.

Animals change as they grow.
The changes are called a **life cycle**.

Puppies start out small.
Their eyes are closed.
They cannot run.
They crawl over each other.

life cycle—changes a living thing goes through while it is alive

hatch—to break out of an egg

larva—a stage in the life cycle of a butterfly before it
becomes a pupa

pupa—a stage in the life cycle of a butterfly that makes
a hard covering

tadpole—a stage in the life cycle of a frog after it hatches
from an egg

They drink milk from their mother.

They grow into dogs.

Some animals grow and change like a puppy.

Baby birds start out in eggs.

They **hatch** when they are big enough.

They use their beaks to break out of the eggs.

Their eyes are open.

They grow more feathers.

They are called chicks.

Chicks grow into birds.

Some animals grow and change like chicks.

Insects change a lot as they grow.
A butterfly is an insect.
It hatches from an egg.
It is called a caterpillar, or **larva**.
The caterpillar eats and eats.
It gets bigger and bigger.

The caterpillar turns into a **pupa**.
It makes a hard covering.
The pupa changes into a butterfly.
It comes out and flies away.

Egg

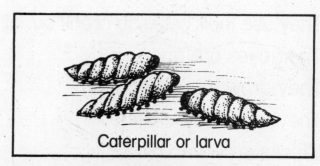

Caterpillar or larva

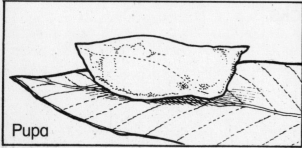

Pupa

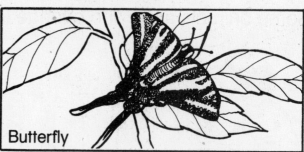

Butterfly

Frogs change a lot as they grow, too.
Young frogs are called **tadpoles**.
They hatch from eggs in water.
Tadpoles have tails.
They have gills to breathe in water.

Lesson 5, Life Cycles of Organisms
Science I, SV 9781419034299

As they grow, tadpoles grow legs.
They get lungs to breathe air.
Their tails get smaller.
Tadpoles turn into frogs.
Frogs live on land.

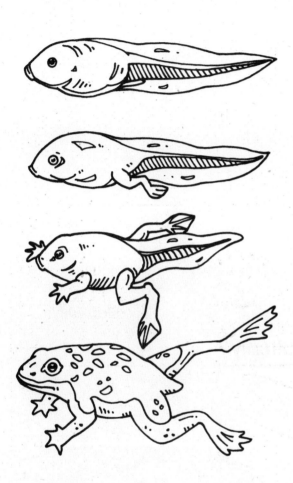

NAME _____   DATE _____

Lesson 5 **Review**

Darken the circle by the best answer.

1. What is an animal's life cycle?

   Ⓐ where the animal lives

   Ⓑ how old the animal is

   Ⓒ how the animal grows and changes

2. What happens when a bird hatches?

   Ⓐ It breaks out of its egg.

   Ⓑ It grows new feathers.

   Ⓒ It finds food.

3. What is the larva in the life cycle of a butterfly?

   Ⓐ when it is an egg

   Ⓑ when it has wings

   Ⓒ when it is a caterpillar

4. How do gills help tadpoles?

   Ⓐ Gills let tadpoles breathe in water.

   Ⓑ Gills help tadpoles jump far on land.

   Ⓒ Gills help tadpoles find food.

Lesson 5, Review
Science 1, SV 9781419034299

Lesson 5   Growing and Changing

Read the clues below. Find the word from the box that matches each clue. Write it on the line under the clue.

chick	life cycle	milk	pupa	tadpole

1. what puppies drink from their mothers

_____

2. the name for a young frog before it lives on land

_____

3. the changes that happen as an animal grows

_____

4. another name for a baby bird

_____

5. what a caterpillar turns into before it becomes a butterfly

_____

                                       Science 1, SV 9781419034299

Lesson 5   **Caterpillars**

**Read the book called <u>The Very Hungry Caterpillar</u>
by Eric Carle.**

**When you are finished, make your own drawings for the book
in the space below. You may want to draw larger pictures on
separate paper and make your own book.**

Lesson 5

Mix and Match

Draw a line from each animal baby to its mother.

1.

a.

2.

b.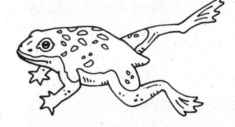

3.

c.

4.

d.

5.

e.

Lesson 5, Mix and Match
Science 1, SV 9781419034299

Lesson 5   **Ostriches**

Read the following passage. Then answer the questions.

One of the biggest eggs in the
world belongs to an ostrich.
The egg can weigh up to 5 pounds.
It is as big as 24 chicken eggs.

The bird that hatches from an ostrich
egg grows very big.
An ostrich is the largest bird there is.
It is also the heaviest.
An ostrich can grow 9 feet tall and
weigh over 300 pounds.

An ostrich cannot fly.
It can run very fast.
An ostrich holds its wings out when it runs.
This helps it to keep from falling.

Ostrich feathers are not like the feathers
of other birds.
Ostrich feathers are very loose and soft.

Ostriches (cont'd.)

~~~~~~

1. Which sentence about an ostrich egg is true?

   (A) It is bigger than a chicken egg.

   (B) It is the same size as a chicken egg.

   (C) It is smaller than a chicken egg.

2. How does an ostrich get away from danger?

   (A) It swims away.

   (B) It flies away.

   (C) It runs very fast.

3. Why do ostriches have wings?

   (A) to keep their balance

   (B) to swim in waves

   (C) to fly through wind

Lesson 5   **Experiment: Butterfly Life Cycle**

What do butterflies look like when they are born?
In this activity, you will study the life cycle of a
butterfly.

What You Will Need

butterfly kit
<u>or</u>
1-liter plastic bottle (empty and clean with top cut off)
piece of screen
leaves
caterpillars

Procedure

1. Set up your butterfly container. If you are not
   using a kit, put leaves in the bottom of the
   bottle. Use screen to make a lid.

2. Add caterpillars to the container. Place the lid
   on the container.

3. Add more leaves every day.

4. Look at the caterpillars every day. Draw a
   picture of them or describe them in words.

5. When you see butterflies, let them go.

Experiment: Butterfly Life Cycle (cont'd.)

Analysis

What happens to the caterpillars after about two weeks?

_____

- - - - - - - - - - - - - - - - - - - -

_____

- - - - - - - - - - - - - - - - - - - -

_____

- - - - - - - - - - - - - - - - - - - -

Conclusion

How do butterflies change as they grow?

_____

- - - - - - - - - - - - - - - - - - - -

_____

- - - - - - - - - - - - - - - - - - - -

_____

- - - - - - - - - - - - - - - - - - - -

Lesson 5, Experiment: Butterfly Life Cycle
Science I, SV 9781419034299

Lesson 6 Organisms and Environments

Think about your home.

You sleep there.

You eat there.

You do many things there.

All animals have homes.

Animal homes are all different.

Forest

A **forest** is a place with many trees.

Some trees grow tall.

Bushes and other plants grow between trees.

Key Terms

forest—a place with many trees

rain forest—a type of forest that is warm and wet

desert—a dry place

ocean—a large body of salt water

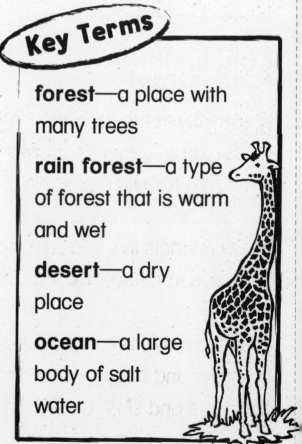

The floor of a forest is shady.
The soil stays wet.

Many animals live in a forest.
Birds live in the branches.
Deer live on the ground.
Worms live in the soil.

Rain Forest

A **rain forest** is a special type of forest.
A rain forest gets rain all year long.
Most rain forests are warm.

Many animals live in a rain forest.
They live in different parts.

Some animals live in the tree branches.
Toucans and macaws are birds that live in trees.
Monkeys and sloths live in trees, too.

Lesson 6, Organisms and Environments
Science I, SV 9781419034299

Some animals live near the forest floor.
Beetles and frogs live there.
So do snails and butterflies.

Desert

A **desert** is a dry place.

There is not much rain.

A desert gets a lot of sunlight.

Many deserts are hot. Others are cold.

Not many plants can live in a desert.

Cactus and yucca plants are desert plants.

Desert plants save water. They use it when
they need it.

Some plants hold water in their stems.

Others have a waxy coat.

Snakes and lizards live in deserts.
So do bobcats and jack rabbits.
Many animals get water from their food.

Some animals stay in the shade when it is hot.
They look for food at night when it is cooler.

Oceans

An **ocean** is a large body of salt water.
About three-fourths of Earth is covered
by oceans.

Oceans are home to many types of plants
and animals.
Some plants float in the water.
Many of these plants are tiny.
You cannot see them with just your eyes.

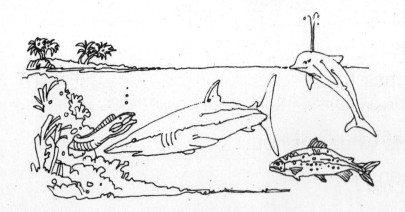

Other plants grow at the bottom.
They grow where the water is not too deep.

Some ocean animals are small.
They drift around in the water.
Jellyfish are these types of animals.

Other ocean animals swim around.
Fish and whales swim in the ocean.
Dolphins swim there, too.

There are some ocean animals that stay
at the bottom.
Lobsters and starfish stay at the bottom.

Lesson 6, Organisms and Environments
Science I, SV 9781419034299

Lesson 6

Review

Darken the circle by the best answer.

1. What would you find in a forest?

   Ⓐ many trees

   Ⓑ lots of sand

   Ⓒ salt water

2. Which words tell about a rain forest?

   Ⓐ cold and dry

   Ⓑ hot and dry

   Ⓒ warm and wet

3. Where would you find a cactus plant?

   Ⓐ desert

   Ⓑ rain forest

   Ⓒ ocean

4. Which animal lives in an ocean?

   Ⓐ deer

   Ⓑ whale

   Ⓒ squirrel

5. About how much of Earth is covered by oceans?

   Ⓐ one-fourth

   Ⓑ one-half

   Ⓒ three-fourths

Lesson 6, Review
Science 1, SV 9781419034299

Lesson 6

Animal Environments

The pictures show different animals. Use the words below to tell where each animal lives. Write the correct word next to each picture.

| forest | rain forest | desert | ocean |

1.

_____

- -

_____

2.

_____

- -

_____

3.

_____

- -

_____

4.

_____

- -

_____

Lesson 6

What Would You Do?

Think about what you would do in each environment.

Would you swing from a tree in the rain forest?

Would you swim on a whale in the ocean?

In the boxes below, draw a picture of what you would do in each environment.

FOREST	RAIN FOREST
DESERT	OCEAN

Lesson 6, What Would You Do?
Science 1, SV 9781419034299

Lesson 6

Cold Desert

Read the following passage. Then answer the questions.

What do you see when you think of a desert?
Do you picture a place that is really hot?
Not all deserts are hot.
Some deserts are cold.

All deserts have one thing in common.
They get less than 50 centimeters of rain or snow
each year.
But, deserts can have very different temperatures.

The temperature in a cold desert is below freezing
in winter.
In summer, the air stays cool.
Cold deserts are found in the Antarctic and in
Greenland.

1. Which sentence about deserts is true?

   (A) All deserts are hot.

   (B) All deserts are cold.

   (C) All deserts are dry.

2. What happens in a cold desert?

   (A) More than 50 centimeters of snow falls each year.

   (B) Less than 50 centimeters of snow falls each year.

   (C) The temperature stays hot all year.

Lesson 6, Cold Desert
Science 1, SV 9781419034299

Lesson 6

Experiment: Animal Habitats

Do animals live in homes?
In this activity, you will find out about
the habitat around you.

What You Will Need

paper
pencil

NOTE: Adult supervision required.

Procedure

1. Visit a place outside at your school or home.

2. Look for animals and plants that live there.

3. Draw pictures of what you see.

4. Visit the place at different times on different
   days. Make notes during each visit.

Analysis

1. What kinds of plants did you see?

_____

- -

_____

Experiment: Animal Habitats (cont'd.)

2. What kinds of animals did you see?

_____

- -

_____

Conclusion

How do the living things you saw get the things
they need to live?

_____

- -

_____

- -

_____

- -

_____

Lesson 6, Experiment: Animal Habitats
Science 1, SV 9781419034299

Lesson 7 Properties of Earth Materials

Rocks are all around you.

You might climb on rocks.

You might throw rocks into water.

People use rocks to make many things.

They use rocks to make buildings, roads, and glass.

They use rocks to make art.

 **Key Terms**

rock—a hard, nonliving thing that comes from Earth

natural resource—something in nature that people can use

mineral—a nonliving thing found in nature

fresh water—water that is not salty

stream—a small body of moving water

river—a body of water that forms from streams that flow together

lake—a body of water that has land all around it

A **rock** is a hard, nonliving thing that comes from Earth.

Some rocks are big and some are small.

Rocks come in different colors.

Some rocks are smooth. Others are rough.

Rocks are one type of natural resource.

A **natural resource** is something in nature that people can use.

There are other natural resources.

The trees in a forest are natural resources.

People use things that grow in trees.

Fruits and nuts grow in trees.

People use wood from trees to make things.

People use wood to make buildings and furniture.

 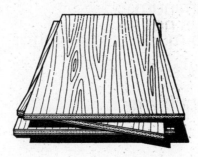

Lesson 7, Properties of Earth Materials
Science I, SV 9781419034299

Soil is another natural resource.

Plants need soil to grow.

People use soil to grow crops for food.

Corn and carrots are crops people grow for food.

Potatoes and lettuce are other crops.

Minerals are another natural resource.

A **mineral** is a nonliving thing found in nature.

Copper and aluminum are minerals.

Many things are made of minerals.

Many cans are made of aluminum.

Some cooking pots are also made of aluminum.

Other pots are made of copper.

Many wires are made of copper, too.

Lesson 7, Properties of Earth Materials
Science 1, SV 9781419034299

Your body uses some minerals.

You get them from your foods.

Calcium and iron are two minerals you need.

Air is all around you.

Air is a natural resource.

You cannot see air.

You can see what air does.

A balloon gets bigger when you blow air into it.

A tree bends when air blows it.

Water is a natural resource.

Fresh water is water that is not salty.

Fresh water comes from rain and snow.

Rain and melted snow flow down mountains.

The water can form a **stream**.

A stream is a small body of moving water.

Lesson 7, Properties of Earth Materials
Science I, SV 9781419034299

A few streams can flow together.

They form a **river**.

A river can flow into a lake.

A **lake** is a body of water that has land all around it.

People need fresh water.

They drink it.

They cook with it.

They use it to clean things.

They wash with it.

People need water to live.

Lesson 7   **Review**

Darken the circle by the best answer.

1. Which of these words does NOT describe a rock?

   (A) hard

   (B) living

   (C) nonliving

2. Which of these is a natural resource?

   (A) trees

   (B) toys

   (C) books

3. How is soil important for many of the foods you eat?

   (A) Soil is food for animals.

   (B) Soil changes into food.

   (C) Crops grow in soil.

4. What are copper, aluminum, and iron?

   (A) minerals

   (B) soils

   (C) crops

5. Where does the water in a stream come from?

   (A) an ocean

   (B) rain and snow

   (C) soil

Lesson 7, Review
Science 1, SV 9781419034299

Lesson 7

Earth's Materials

Fill in the puzzle with the words described by each clue.
Choose from the word box.

| crops | lake | rock | soil |
| fresh | resource | stream | |

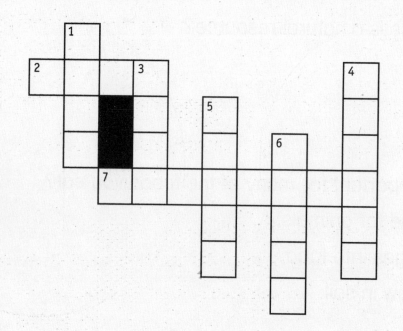

Across

2. something plants need to grow in
7. something from nature that people can use

Down

1. a hard, nonliving thing
3. a body of water that has land all around it
4. a small body of moving water
5. plants used for food, such as corn and potatoes
6. water that is not salty

Lesson 7, Earth's Materials
Science I, SV 9781419034299

Lesson 7   **A Rock Collection**

Find a small collection of rocks near your home or school.

Look at each rock carefully.

Put the rocks into a few groups.

Use the circles below to show each group.

Explain why you put each rock into its group.

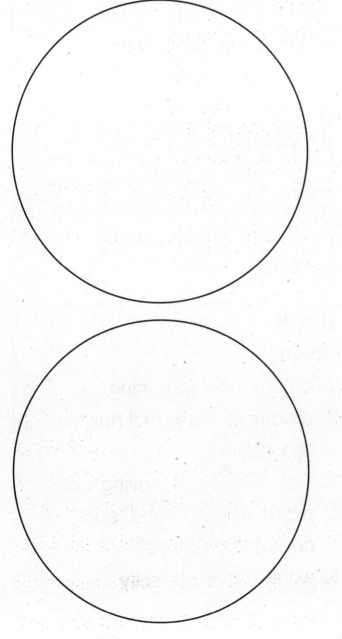
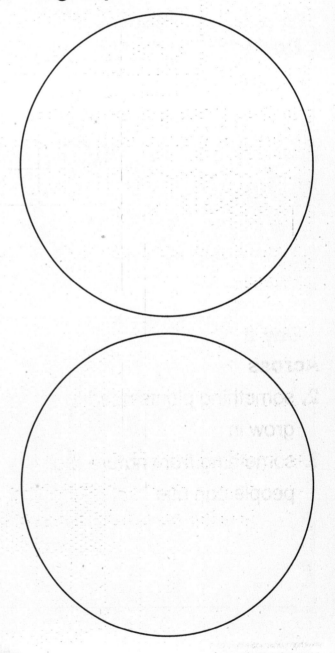

Lesson 7, A Rock Collection
Science 1, SV 9781419034299

Lesson 7

Plants on the Menu

Some of the foods you eat come from plants.
Fruits and vegetables come from plants.
Grains and rice come from plants, too.

Write down what you eat for lunch for four days.
Circle the foods that come from plants.
Tell a friend or family member why soil is important.

Day 1	Day 2
Day 3	**Day 4**

Lesson 7

All About Air

Air is all around you.

Think of four ways that you can see what air does.

Does it help you fly a kite?

Does it help you blow up a balloon?

Does it make a boat sail?

Draw pictures showing four ways that you can see what air does.

Lesson 7   Growing Plants Without Soil

Read the following passage. Then answer the questions.

Soil is an important natural resource.

Sometimes there is not enough good soil.

That is why some plants are grown without soil.

They are grown in water.

Growing plants in water is good in several ways.

It does not use lots of land.

The plants are given what they need in their water.

There are no weeds to pull.

The plants grow faster than plants grown in soil.

The plants can be grown indoors.

1. What resource is saved by growing plants in
   water?

   (A) air

   (B) soil

   (C) water

2. How do plants grown in water get what they need?

   (A) They need to take in some soil.

   (B) They get it from air.

   (C) It is put into their water.

Lesson 7   **Experiment: A River Model**

Rivers form from rain and melted snow.
In this activity, you will make a river.

What You Will Need

clay
board
water
sand or soil

Procedure

1. Use clay to make a mountain on the board.

2. With your finger, carve out a path for a river.

3. Make streams flowing into the river.

4. Cover the mountain with a thin layer of sand or
   soil.

5. Pour a small amount of water at the top of the
   mountain. Watch how the water flows.

Analysis

1. Did the water flow faster near the top of the
   mountain or at the bottom?

   _____

   -

   _____

Experiment: A River Model (cont'd.)

2. Did your river flow straight, or did it curve?

_____

- -

_____

Conclusion

How might a river carry sand or soil from one
place to another?

_____

- -

_____

- -

_____

Lesson 8 Objects in the Sky

What do you see in the sky at night?

You might see stars.

A **star** is an object in the sky that gives off light.

There are many stars in the sky.

They are very far from Earth.

One important star is the sun.

The **sun** is the closest star to Earth.

You can see the sun during the day.

You cannot see the sun at night.

Key Terms

star—an object in the sky that gives off light

sun—the closest star to Earth

moon—a rock that moves around Earth

At night you may see the moon.
The **moon** is a huge rock that moves
around Earth.
It is the brightest thing in the night sky.
The moon does not make its own light.
It is lit by the sun.

www.harcourtschoolsupply.com
96
Lesson 8, Objects in the Sky
Science I, SV 9781419034299

Earth is a planet.

Mars and Venus are two other planets.

These planets are made of rock.

On some nights, you may see Mars and Venus.

Lesson 8, Objects in the Sky
Science 1, SV 9781419034299

Lesson 8

Review

Darken the circle by the best answer.

1. What is the sun?

   (A) a planet

   (B) a star

   (C) a moon

2. Why does the moon light up at night?

   (A) It is lit by lights on Earth.

   (B) It burns like a fire.

   (C) Sunlight hits it.

3. What is the moon made of?

   (A) rock

   (B) water

   (C) cheese

4. Which of these is NOT a planet?

   (A) Mars

   (B) the sun

   (C) Venus

Lesson 8

Twinkle, Twinkle

Write a short poem about a star.

The poem does not have to rhyme.

It has to tell what you think about stars.

Start by writing words that describe stars.

Then put the words into sentences to write your poem.

_____

Words: _____

_____

_____

_____

Poem: _____

_____

_____

_____

_____

Lesson 8, Twinkle, Twinkle
Science 1, SV 9781419034299

Lesson 8

Life Cycle of a Star

Read the following passage. Then answer the questions.

Stars are not living things.

Even so, they go through a life cycle.

They are born.

They live.

In time, stars die.

Stars begin from dust and gas in space.

They squeeze together to form a young star.

A young star is called a protostar.

A young star squeezes together even more.

It turns into a star that lives for billions of years.

A star gets bigger when it gets old.

It runs out of the fuel that made it glow.

It becomes cool and not as bright.

Then the star explodes.

Life Cycle of a Star (cont'd.)

1. Which sentence about stars is true?

(A) Stars are living things.

(B) Stars are nonliving things.

(C) Stars never change.

2. What is a protostar?

(A) a young star

(B) a dead star

(C) a picture of a star

3. How long does a star live?

(A) one year

(B) one hundred years

(C) several billion years

4. What causes a star to die?

(A) It runs out of fuel.

(B) It crashes into another star.

(C) It makes a new star.

Lesson 8   **Experiment: By the Light of the Moon**

You can see the moon at night.

The moon does not make light.

In this activity, you will find out how you can see

the moon at night.

What You Will Need

a partner

large ball

small ball

flashlight

Procedure

1. Place a flashlight on a desk or table.
   Turn it on. This is the sun.

2. Have your partner hold a large ball.
   This is Earth.

3. Hold a smaller ball near Earth.
   This is the moon.

4. Dim the lights.

5. Move the moon around Earth.

6. Watch to see how the moon is lit up
   from the sun.

Experiment: By the Light of the Moon (cont'd.)

Analysis

1. When was the moon lit up from the sun?

_____

- -

_____

2. What makes the moon light up?

_____

- -

_____

Conclusion

How can a person see the moon at night?

_____

- -

_____

_____

- -

Lesson 9 Changes in Earth and Sky

You go to bed at night.
You wake up in the morning.

Night is different from day.
It is dark at night.
It is light during the day. The sun shines.
Night is cooler than day.
The sun's heat warms land, air, and water
during the day.

Key Terms

rotate—to spin in a circle

season—a time of the year

winter—the season after fall that has cold air and short days

spring—the season after winter when plants begin to grow and many animals are born

summer—the season after spring that has warm air and long days

fall—the season after summer when some trees lose their leaves

Day and night happen because Earth moves.

Earth **rotates**.

This means it spins like a top.

Earth rotates one time every 24 hours.

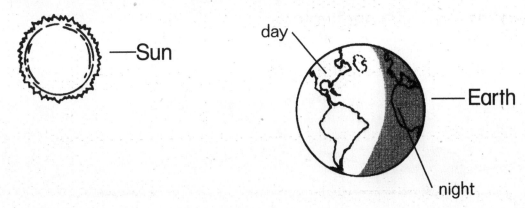

—Sun

day

—Earth

night

The sun shines on half of Earth.
This side of Earth has day.

The other half of Earth is dark.
This side of Earth has night.

As Earth rotates, the part that was in the sunlight
moves into darkness.
It changes from day to night.
The other part moves from darkness into sunlight.
It changes from night to day.

Earth moves in another way.
It moves around the sun.

In some places, part of Earth points
toward the sun.
Other places point away from the sun.
This causes seasons.
A **season** is a time of the year.
The seasons are spring, summer, fall, and winter.

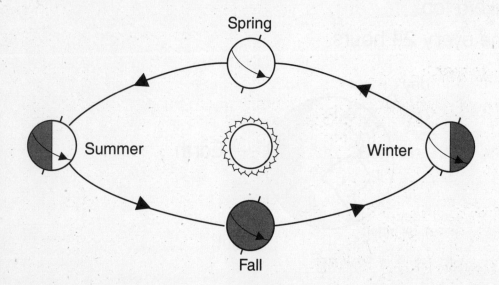

Spring

Summer

Winter

Fall

Winter is the coldest season.
It has fewer hours of daylight than any other season.
In some places, snow falls in winter.

Some trees do not have leaves in winter.
Some plants die in winter.

Lesson 9, Changes in Earth and Sky
Science I, SV 9781419034299

Animals need to keep warm in winter.
Some animals sleep through the winter.
Other animals move to warmer places until
winter is over.

Spring comes after winter.
There are more hours of daylight.
The air gets warmer.
There is more rain.

Many plants start growing in spring.
Some animals have babies in the spring.

Summer comes after spring.
Summer has more hours of sunlight than
any other season.
In many places, the air gets hot.

Lesson 9, Changes in Earth and Sky
Science I, SV 9781419034299

Most plants grow well in summer.
They grow leaves and flowers.
They also make fruits.
Young animals grow during summer.

Fall follows summer.
There are not as many hours of sunlight
as in summer.
The leaves of some trees change colors.
Then they fall to the ground.

With less sunlight, plants stop growing bigger.
Fruits and vegetables are picked.
Some animals store food for winter.

Lesson 9   **Review**

Darken the circle by the best answer.

1. How do you move when you rotate?
   - (A) climb stairs
   - (B) run in a line
   - (C) spin in a circle

2. Which of these happens because Earth rotates?
   - (A) seasons
   - (B) day and night
   - (C) ocean waves

3. Which of these is the coldest season?
   - (A) winter
   - (B) summer
   - (C) spring

4. In which season do many plants start growing?
   - (A) summer
   - (B) spring
   - (C) fall

5. In which season do many trees lose their leaves?
   - (A) summer
   - (B) spring
   - (C) fall

Lesson 9

Changes in the Sky

Write words to complete the sentences. Choose from the words in the box.

```
day      rotates    sun
night    season
```

_____

1. Earth _____ by spinning like a top.

2. A _____ is a time of the year.

3. Earth moves around the _____.

4. People are in the dark at _____.

5. Part of Earth receives sunlight during the _____.

Lesson 9   The Seasons

Seasons are different around the world.

Each box below is for one season.

In the box, draw something you do in that season.

Maybe you swim in summer.

Perhaps you make snowballs in winter.

SPRING	SUMMER
FALL	**WINTER**

Lesson 9

Time Zones

Read the following passage. Then answer the questions.

It is day in the United States.

It is night in Japan.

It cannot be the same time in both places.

If it was, the same time of day would be very
different in each place.

To prevent this, Earth has 24 times zones.

Each zone has a different time.

Things are the same at each time no matter
where it is.

The sun is highest at noon.

The time 9:00 A.M. is in the morning.

The time 9:00 P.M. is at night.

There is a pretend line that goes from
top to bottom halfway around Earth.

It shows where the date changes.

It is one day on one side of the line.

It is the next day on the other side of the line.

This line is called the International Date Line.

1. Which sentence is true?

   Ⓐ It is the same time all over Earth.

   Ⓑ There are 24 different times on Earth.

   Ⓒ Every city has a different time.

2. What happens at noon?

   Ⓐ The date changes.

   Ⓑ The sun does not shine.

   Ⓒ The sun is highest in the sky.

3. Why are there 24 time zones?

   Ⓐ There are 24 hours in a day.

   Ⓑ There are 24 minutes in an hour.

   Ⓒ There are 24 days in a month.

Lesson 9, Time Zones
Science 1, SV 9781419034299

Lesson 9
Experiment: Sunrise to Sunset

Day begins at sunrise.

Night begins at sunset.

In this activity, you will learn about sunrise and sunset.

What You Will Need

large ball or globe

flashlight

sticky note

an adult helper

Procedure

1. Place a flashlight on a desk or table. Turn it on.

2. Find your town on the globe. Put a sticky note on it.

3. Dim the lights. Turn the globe so that your town is in the dark.

4. Ask an adult to help you turn the globe in a counterclockwise direction.

5. Stop turning when your town is in the light. This is point A.

6. Start turning the globe again.

7. Stop when the town is back in the dark. This is point B.

Experiment: Sunrise to Sunset (cont'd.)

Analysis

1. At which point did sunrise happen?

_____

- -

_____

2. What happened at Point B?

_____

- -

_____

Conclusion

How long does it take for your town to move from
Point A all the way back to Point A?

_____

- -

_____

Lesson 9, Experiment: Sunrise to Sunset
Science 1, SV 9781419034299

Science Fair Projects

You can learn about nature.
A science fair project can help.

Pick a Topic

Pick what you want to learn about.
You might pick animals or plants.
You might pick rocks.
What you pick is your topic.

Ask a question about your topic.
You might ask what rocks are made of.
You might ask how clouds make weather.

Find Information

Find out about your topic.
Look in books.
Look in magazines.
Use the Internet.

Talk to people about the topic.

You might ask a dentist about teeth.

You might ask a gardener about growing plants.

Types of Projects

There are three types of projects.

An Experiment

An experiment is a test you do.

It will help you answer your question.

You begin with a guess.

You guess the answer to your question.

Then pick a way to test your guess.

You may want to know if plant food helps plants grow.

You might guess that it does.

Grow two plants.

Add plant food to one.

Science Fair Projects
Science I, SV 9781419034299

Look at the plants every day.
Write down how each one looks.

Think about what you saw.
Try to figure out what it means.

Decide what happened.
You might decide that the plant
with food grew better.

You find out if your guess was right.
Sometimes it is right. Sometimes it is not.
Either way, you learn from your test.

An Exhibit
Some science projects are models.
They show things in nature.
A model can show planets.

Other projects are demonstrations.
They show how things happen.
One might show what a volcano does.

A Collection
A collection is a group of things.
The things should be from nature.
They might be rocks or leaves.

Science Fair Projects
Science 1, SV 9781419034299

You put the things into groups.
You put things that are the same into a group.
You put things that are not the same into different groups.

You might group rocks by their color.
You might group leaves by their shape

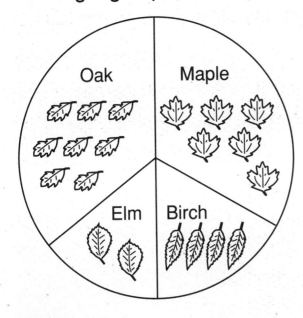

Safety

You need to stay safe during your project.
Listen to your teacher or parent.

Ask your teacher or parent before you start.
Tell your teacher or parent if something breaks
or spills.

Wear safety goggles.
Tie back long hair.
Do not wear loose clothing.
Do not eat or drink while you do your project.

Science Fair Projects
Science I, SV 9781419034299

Presenting the Project

Show what you learned.

Make a display.

Your display should tell about your project.

It should be neat.

Write the title of your project.

Print your name.

Write your teacher's name.

Write the date.

Tell why you did the project.

List the things you used.

Write the steps you followed.

Show the drawings you made.

Paste the photos you took.

Write what you did and saw.

Make graphs and charts when you can.

Tell what you found out.

Tell if your guess was right.

List the books you used.

List magazines and newspapers.

List the people you asked.

Science Fair Projects
Science I, SV 9781419034299

Project Ideas

Here are some ideas to think about.
You might use one of them.
They might help you think of another idea.

- **What happens to water that is left out in the sun?** Take pictures of a puddle over time. Explain what happens to it.

- **What are everyday examples of solids, liquids, and gases?** Show pictures of matter in different states. Tell how one state is different from another.

- **Does salt water freeze faster than plain water?** Add the same amounts of salt water and plain water to different containers. Put the containers in the freezer. Check the containers to find out which one freezes first. Tell what this means about the liquids.

- **Which objects move fast? Which move slowly?** Put a number of objects in order by their speed.

- **What are some uses for magnets?** Show different kinds of magnets. Tell where and how they are used.

Science Fair Projects
Science 1, SV 9781419034299

- **What things are pulled to a magnet?** Test many different items. Show which ones are pulled to the magnet and which ones are not.

- **Is the temperature of air the same in the sun and in the shade?** Measure air temperature at different places at the same time.

- **How can light be moved by mirrors?** Show how light can be bounced off mirrors to move around an object.

- **What can you do with static electricity?** Use static electricity to bend a stream of water or pick up bits of tissue paper.

- **What things are alive?** Prepare a display of living and nonliving things. Explain the difference between them.

- **How do different conditions affect how fast fruits ripen?** Change the conditions for several pieces of fruit. For example, place some in the refrigerator, some in bags, and some in sunlight. Check them each day to find out which get ripe first.

- **Do seeds grow better at different depths in the soil?** Fill several containers with soil. In one container, put seeds deep into the soil.

Science Fair Projects
Science I, SV 9781419034299

In another, put seeds a little below the surface. In another, place seeds at the top. Find out which seeds become seedlings first.

- **What are the parts of a hen's egg?** Show the parts of an egg. Tell what each part does.

- **What types of living things can be found around the world?** Show types of living things in different environments or in your local environment.

- **How much of Earth is covered by land?** How much is covered by water? Make a map and label water and land.

- **What things are on other planets?** Describe things on other planets. Tell which planets have volcanoes. Show which planets have moons.

- **How do the planets move?** Show how the planets spin and how they move around the sun.

- **What causes day and night?** Tell how day and night are different on other planets.

Glossary

attract—to pull together (p. 33)

change—to make different (p. 7)

circuit—a path that electricity flows through (p. 33)

curve—a bend (p. 22)

desert—a dry place (p. 70)

dissolve—to mix with a liquid (p. 7)

energy—the ability to make things change (p. 33)

fall—the season after summer when some trees lose their leaves (p. 104)

float—to stay on top of a liquid (p. 7)

force—a push or a pull (p. 22)

forest—a place with many trees (p. 70)

fresh water—water that is not salty (p. 82)

friction—a force that acts against motion (p. 22)

gas—matter that does not have its own shape or size (p. 7)

hatch—to break out of an egg (p. 58)

lake—a body of water that has land all around it (p. 82)

larva—a stage in the life cycle of a butterfly before it becomes a pupa (p. 58)

life cycle—changes a living thing goes through while it is alive (p. 58)

liquid—matter that flows (p. 7)

living thing—something that grows and changes (p. 45)

matter—everything around you (p. 7)

mineral—a nonliving thing found in nature (p. 82)

moon—a rock that moves around Earth (p. 95)

motion—moving from one place to another (p. 22)

natural resource—something in nature that people can use (p. 82)

Glossary, page 2

nonliving thing—something that does not grow and change (p. 45)

ocean—a large body of salt water (p. 70)

organism—a living thing (p. 45)

pole—a place where a magnet is strongest (p. 33)

pupa—a stage in the life cycle of a butterfly that makes a hard covering (p. 58)

rain forest—a type of forest that is warm and wet (p. 70)

repel—to push apart (p. 33)

river—a body of water that forms from streams that flow together (p. 82)

rock—a hard, nonliving thing that comes from Earth (p. 82)

rotate—to spin in a circle (p. 104)

season—a time of the year (p. 104)

senses—smelling, touching, seeing, tasting, and hearing (p. 45)

sink—to drop to the bottom of a liquid (p. 7)

solid—matter that keeps its shape (p. 7)

speed—how fast or slow an object moves (p. 22)

spring—the season after winter when plants begin to grow and many animals are born (p. 104)

star—an object in the sky that gives off light (p. 95)

stream—a small body of moving water (p. 82)

summer—the season after spring that has warm air and long days (p. 104)

sun—the closest star to Earth (p. 95)

surface—the top or outside of something (p. 22)

tadpole—a stage in the life cycle of a frog after it hatches from an egg (p. 58)

winter—the season after fall that has cold air and short days (p. 104)

Glossary
Science I, SV 9781419034299

Answer Key

Assessment, pp. 5-6
1. B	2. A	3. B
4. B	5. A	6. C
7. A	8. A	9. A

Unit 1 Lesson 1
Review, p. 14

1. C   2. B   3. A   4. C   5. C

Kinds of Matter, p. 15
1. g	2. d	3. h	4. c
5. b	6. f	7. e	8. a

Float or Sink, p. 16
1. float	2. float
3. sink	4. sink

Submarines, p. 18
1. C   2. B   3. C   4. A

Experiment: Which One Floats on Top?, pp. 20–21
Analysis

1. corn syrup
2. water
3. vegetable oil

Conclusion

1. Corn syrup was the heaviest.
2. Vegetable oil was the lightest.
3. No. The layers would be the same.

Unit 1 Lesson 2
Review, p. 27

1. B   2. C   3. A   4. B   5. C

Types of Motion, p. 28
1. curve	2. straight
3. zigzag	4. back and forth
5. spin	

Comparing Surfaces, p. 29
Students should use descriptive words to tell how each surface feels. The car should travel the farthest on the smoothest surface. It should travel the shortest distance on the roughest surface.

Curling, p. 30
1. C   2. B

Experiment: Making Things Move, p. 32
Analysis

1. It stretched more without the pencils.
2. The wheels are like the pencils.

Conclusion You need to use less force to slide something when you roll it on wheels.

Unit 1 Lesson 3
Review, p. 38

1. B   2. C   3. A   4. B   5. C

All About Energy, p. 39
1. energy	2. bend
3. Heat	4. battery
5. circuit	6. poles

Lights All Around, p. 40
Check student drawings. Encourage students to look around for additional examples.

Magnetic Forces, p. 41
1. repel (arrows opposite directions)
2. attract (arrows toward each other)

Magnetic Trains, p. 43
1. C   2. A   3. B

Experiment: Bending Light, p. 44
Analysis   The foam cup blocked light bouncing off the penny.

Answer Key
Science I, SV 9781419034299

Answer Key cont'd.

Conclusion Water bent light so that I could see the penny.

Unit 2 Lesson 4
Review, p. 51
1. C   2. C   3. A   4. B   5. A

Sensing Your Surroundings, p. 52
Check student examples for accuracy.

Alive or Not, p. 53
1. living   2. nonliving
3. nonliving   4. living
5. living   6. nonliving

Sounds Animals Hear, pp. 54–55
1. B   2. A   3. C   4. B

Experiment: Using Your Senses, p. 57
Analysis   Students should list which senses they used to guess what each object is.
Conclusion All of the senses get information about an object. If one sense is not used, the others fill in.

Unit 2 Lesson 5
Review, p. 62
1. C   2. A   3. C   4. A

Growing and Changing, p. 63
1. milk   2. tadpole
3. life cycle   4. chick
5. pupa

Caterpillars, p. 64
Accept all drawings that show change over time.

Mix and Match, p. 65
1. d   2. c   3. e   4. b   5. a

Ostriches, p. 67
1. A   2. C   3. A

Experiment: Butterfly Life Cycle, p. 69
Analysis   They form a closed structure (called a chrysalis).
Conclusion They begin as eggs that become caterpillars that develop into butterflies.

Unit 2 Lesson 6
Review, p. 75
1. A   2. C   3. A   4. B   5. C

Animal Environments, p. 76
1. ocean   2. desert
3. rain forest   4. forest

What Would You Do?, p. 77
Accept all drawings.

Cold Desert, p. 79
1. C   2. B

Experiment: Animal Habitats, pp. 80–81
Analysis   Answers will vary.
Conclusion Answers will vary. Students might say that animals eat plants, birds live in nests in trees, and trees grow in soil.

Unit 3 Lesson 7
Review, p. 87
1. B   2. A   3. C   4. A   5. B

Answer Key cont'd.

Earth's Materials, p. 88
Across
2. soil   7. resource
Down
1. rock   3. lake
4. stream   5. crops
6. fresh

A Rock Collection, p. 89
Students should divide rocks into groups according to their characteristics, such as size, color, shape, or hardness.

Plants on the Menu, p. 90
Students should identify foods that originate from plants.

All About Air, p. 91
Students should be creative when drawing examples. All examples should involve air or wind in some way.

Growing Plants Without Soil, p. 92
1. B   2. C

Experiment: A River Model, pp. 93–94
Analysis
1. The water should flow faster near the top.
2. Answers will vary.
Conclusion Sand or soil at the top of the mountain might flow with the water to the bottom.

Unit 3 Lesson 8
Review, p. 98
1. B   2. C   3. A   4. B

Twinkle, Twinkle, p. 99
Accept all answers. Encourage students to be creative.

Life Cycle of a Star, p. 101
1. B   2. A   3. C   4. A

Experiment: By the Light of the Moon, p. 103
Analysis
1. when the flashlight shone on it
2. The sun lights the moon.
Conclusion The person is on the side of Earth opposite to the sun. The moon is lit up by the sun. The person can see this light.

Unit 3 Lesson 9
Review, p. 109
1. C   2. B   3. A   4. B   5. C

Changes in the Sky, p. 110
1. rotates   2. season
3. sun   4. night
5. day

The Seasons, p. 111
Check that student drawings match the seasons in your region.

Time Zones, p. 113
1. B   2. C   3. A

Experiment: Sunrise to Sunset, p. 115
Analysis
1. Point A   2. sunset
Conclusion 1 day, or 24 hours